KNOW YOUR WORTH IN LIFE

Unlocking Your Purpose and Living with Passion, Strength, and Resilience

JASON SMITH

KNOW YOUR WORTH in Life: Unlocking Your Divine Purpose and Living with Spiritual Strength and Resilience

Copyright © 2024 by Jason Smith

All rights reserved.

This book is protected under copyright law. No portion of this publication may be reproduced, distributed, or transmitted in any form or by any means—including electronic, mechanical, photocopying, recording, or other methods—without the express written consent of the publisher, except for brief excerpts used in critical reviews or articles.

This work is a nonfiction book based on the author's personal experiences, insights, and reflections. While the events and narratives shared are true to the author's life, any resemblance to individuals, living or deceased, or to specific events is unintentional and coincidental.

Published by Day-N-Night Publishing, LLC

Cover Design: Jason Smith

ISBN: 979-8-9905788-5-2

Library of Congress: 2025909670

Printed in the United States of America

First Edition: 2025

For permission requests or other inquiries, please contact:

PO Box 939

Ellabell, GA 31308

❦ Created with Vellum

Dedication

With a heart full of gratitude, I dedicate this book to God, my Creator and Sustainer. In every trial and every tear, You have been my unwavering strength, my guiding light, and my enduring source of hope. Your grace and love have carried me through the darkest times, reminding me that I am never alone, even when facing the deepest struggles. Thank you for always being by my side, revealing my worth and purpose through moments of hardship.

To my mother, your unconditional love and support have been my anchor in life's storms. You believed in me when I struggled to believe in myself, and your encouragement gave me the strength to keep going. Thank you for being my rock and for showing me what true resilience looks like.

To my close friend, you stood by me when I needed it most, offering a listening ear, a helping hand, and a heart full of compassion. Your friendship has been a gift I will forever cherish, and I am so grateful for your presence in my life.

To the remarkable people who stood by me during my most challenging season, this book is also for you. To those who believed in me, offered words of encouragement, and reminded me that my circumstances didn't define my worth, I am deeply thankful. Your kindness, support, and prayers lifted me when I felt I could not continue.

I want to take a moment to reflect on the difficult year I spent living in my truck after being evicted. It was a time that tested my faith, resilience, and determination in ways I never anticipated. To those who encountered me during that period and chose to uplift rather than judge, you showed me true compassion. Your humanity gave me the courage to keep pushing forward despite the challenges.

I also want to express my appreciation to the union where I fought hard to survive during that year. Thank you for providing me with an opportunity to move ahead, even when the odds felt insurmountable. Those long days of work taught me the genuine meaning of perseverance and grit.

This book stands as a testimony to what God can accomplish when we remain faithful, even amid struggles. It serves as proof that no matter how low you may feel, there is always a path forward. To everyone who played a role in my journey, no matter how significant or small, I am forever grateful. Your impact will always be a cherished part of my story.

And to anyone out there who feels lost or defeated—please remember, your story is not finished. God is with you, and your worth is far greater than you can imagine. Keep moving forward; there is hope ahead.

With heartfelt gratitude and love

TABLE OF CONTENTS

INTRODUCTION	1
The Journey to Knowing Your Worth	1
PART ONE: UNDERSTANDING PURPOSE	4
P – Positioning Yourself for God's Plan	
Understanding God's Plan	4
Clearing Distractions	5
Spiritual Practices for Alignment	6
CHAPTER TWO	10
U – Understanding Your Identity in Christ	
Knowing Who You Are in God	10
Breaking Free from Worldly Labels	13
Embracing Your Spiritual Gifts	13
PART TWO: RECOGNIZING AND PURSUING YOUR PURPOSE	17
R – Recognizing Your Calling	
Signs of Your God-Given Calling	17
Recognizing God's Voice	18
Overcoming Barriers to Recognizing Your Calling	22
CHAPTER FOUR	24
P – Pursuing Purpose with Passion	
Finding Passion in Your Work	24
Overcoming Fear and Procrastination	25
Trusting God in Every Season	28
PART THREE: LIVING OUT YOUR PURPOSE	32
O – Overcoming Obstacles with Faith	
Developing Spiritual Resilience	33
Examples of Overcoming Obstacles in Scripture	36
Faith Overcomes All	38
CHAPTER SIX	39
S – Stepping Out in Boldness	
Confronting Fear and Insecurities	39
The Biblical Call to Boldness	40
Confronting Fear and Doubt	41

Practical Steps to Step Out in Boldness	42
Walk Boldly into Your Destiny	45
CHAPTER SEVEN	46
E—Embracing Your Eternal Impact	
Living for Legacy, Not Just Success	46
Leaving a Legacy of Faith and Love	48
Eternal Impact in Your Sphere of Influence	51
The Eternal Reward	52
Shine Bright for Eternity	52
LIVING A LIFE OF WORTH	53
Living Your Purpose, Knowing Your Worth	54
A Call to Rise	54
The Invitation to Salvation	55
A Prayer of Salvation	55
Next Steps in Your Faith Journey	56
Walking in Your P.U.R.P.O.S.E	56
A FINAL WORD OF ENCOURAGEMENT	58
Afterword	59
Acknowledgments	61

INTRODUCTION

THE JOURNEY TO KNOWING YOUR WORTH

Have you ever felt like you're merely going through the motions, unsure of your purpose? Do you wrestle with self-doubt, questioning whether you're truly meant for more? If so, you're not alone. Many people grapple with these same feelings of being lost, unfulfilled, or stuck in a cycle of uncertainty.

The truth is you were created with a divine purpose. Your existence is no accident. God has a unique plan for your life—one filled with meaning, passion, and impact. But to step into that purpose, you must first understand your worth.

Why We Struggle

Many of us face frustration and hardship because we are not aligned with our God-given purpose. Instead of following the path He has laid out for us, we often chase after things that were never meant for us. We seek validation from the world, choose comfort over calling, and allow fear to dictate our decisions. However, when we discover our true worth in Christ, everything changes.

- We stop settling for less than we deserve.
- We gain clarity about our mission in life.
- We walk in confidence, knowing we are equipped and called by God.

The P.U.R.P.O.S.E. Framework

This book is structured around the word P.U.R.P.O.S.E., guiding you through seven key principles to help you unlock your worth and live with confidence and resilience:

1. **P** – Positioning Yourself for God's Plan – Surrendering to His will and creating space for divine guidance.
2. **U** – Understanding Your Identity in Christ – Recognizing your God-given value and gifts.
3. **R** – Recognizing Your Calling – Discovering how God speaks through your passions and experiences.
4. **P** – Pursuing Purpose with Passion – Overcoming fear and walking boldly in your calling.
5. **O** – Overcoming Obstacles with Faith – Trusting God through challenges and setbacks.
6. **S** – Stepping Out in Boldness – Taking action with confidence and courage.
7. **E** – Embracing Your Eternal Impact – Living with purpose beyond yourself, leaving a legacy of faith.

EACH CHAPTER WILL CHALLENGE YOU TO REFLECT DEEPLY ON YOUR spiritual journey and take actionable steps toward embracing your purpose. Along the way, you'll find scripture, real-life examples, and practical guidance to help you grow in faith and confidence.

It's Time to Step Into Your Purpose

God is calling you to more. He has placed unique gifts, talents, and dreams within you for a reason. The struggles and setbacks you've faced are not meant to break you but to prepare you for something greater.

This book is your invitation to stop living beneath your worth and start walking in your God-ordained purpose. It's time to rise, step into your calling, and live with passion, strength, and resilience.

LET'S BEGIN

PART ONE: UNDERSTANDING PURPOSE
P – POSITIONING YOURSELF FOR GOD'S PLAN

The journey to discovering your worth begins with aligning yourself with God's divine plan. This process requires intentional surrender, eliminating distractions, and fostering an environment that nurtures spiritual growth. At its heart, positioning yourself for God's plan means embracing the truth of Jeremiah 29:11, which assures us of God's good intentions:

"For I know the plans I have for you," declares the Lord, *"plans to prosper you and not to harm you, plans to give you hope and a future."*

IN THIS CHAPTER, WE WILL EXPLORE PRACTICAL STEPS TO POSITION yourself for God's purposes. From creating space for God to work in your life through prayer and fasting to surrounding yourself with spiritually uplifted and challenged people, this chapter will guide you toward greater clarity and intimacy with God.

UNDERSTANDING GOD'S PLAN

One of the most profound truths in Scripture is that God has a specific plan for each of us. Yet, many struggle to believe this due to life's uncertainties, disappointments, or a lack of direction. The first step in positioning yourself for His plan is embracing the certainty that God is intentional in His design for your life.

Why Positioning Matters

Positioning yourself for God's plan is not just about being in the right place physically but adopting the correct spiritual posture. This involves:

- Letting go of your own agenda.
- Trusting God's timing and methods, even when they don't align with your expectations.
- Acknowledging that God's ways are higher than yours (Isaiah 55:8-9).

When you position yourself spiritually, you become like clay in the hands of the Potter (Jeremiah 18:6), ready for Him to shape and mold you according to His will.

CLEARING DISTRACTIONS

One of the greatest barriers to fulfilling God's plan is distractions that pull our focus away from Him. These distractions can take many forms, including busyness, unhealthy relationships, misplaced priorities, and even our own fears and insecurities.

Identifying Distractions

To begin clearing distractions, it's essential to identify what is pulling you away from God. Ask yourself:

- What occupies most of my thoughts during the day?
- Are there habits or activities in my life that hinder my spiritual growth?
- Do my relationships draw me closer to God or pull me further from Him?

Steps to Clear Distractions

- EVALUATE YOUR PRIORITIES
    - Make a list of the things that dominate your time and energy. Prayerfully ask God to reveal which aligns with His will and which needs to be removed or adjusted.
- SET BOUNDARIES:
    - Setting boundaries is crucial to maintaining focus on God. This might mean limiting time on social media, stepping back from toxic relationships, or saying no to commitments that drain you.
- PRACTICE SOLITUDE:
    - Jesus often withdrew to lonely places to pray (Luke 5:16). Taking time away from the noise of life to be alone with God allows you to refocus and hear His voice more clearly.

SPIRITUAL PRACTICES FOR ALIGNMENT

"The Power of Prayer and Fasting"

Prayer and fasting are essential tools for preparing for God's plan. They deepen your relationship with God and provide clarity and guidance for the path ahead.

Why Prayer is Foundational

Prayer is a believer's lifeline. Through prayer, we communicate with God, seek His will, and align our hearts with His purposes.

Listening in Prayer:

Prayer is not just about presenting requests to God; it's also about listening. Quieting your heart creates space for God to speak.

Persistent Prayer:

The scripture urges us to pray continually (1 Thessalonians 5:17). This involves staying consistently aware of God's presence in your daily life.

Fasting for Spiritual Clarity

Fasting is a spiritual discipline that helps you disconnect from worldly distractions and focus on God. Whether it's fasting from food, social media, or other distractions, the purpose is to draw nearer to God.

Biblical Examples of Fasting:

Many biblical figures, including Jesus, fasted before making significant decisions or embarking on ministry. For example, Jesus fasted for 40 days in the wilderness before beginning His public ministry (Matthew 4:1-2).

Practical Tips for Fasting:

If you're new to fasting, begin gradually by skipping a single meal and using that time for prayer.

Combine fasting with prayer for maximum spiritual benefit.

Focus on the purpose of the fast, not the physical discomfort.

Surrounding Yourself with the Right People

The people you surround yourself with can either propel you toward God's plan or pull you away. Scripture emphasizes the importance of godly relationships:

"As iron sharpens iron, so one person sharpens another." — Proverbs 27:17

Characteristics of Godly Relationships

ENCOURAGEMENT

Friends who encourage you in your faith journey can help you stay focused on God's plan, even during challenging times.

ACCOUNTABILITY

It is invaluable to have people in your life who will lovingly hold you accountable for your commitments and spiritual growth.

WISDOM

Surround yourself with spiritually mature individuals who can offer godly counsel when you face decisions or challenges.

Pruning Unhealthy Relationships

JUST AS A GARDENER PRUNES BRANCHES TO ENCOURAGE GROWTH, sometimes we must let go of relationships that hinder our walk with God. This doesn't mean abandoning people, but it may involve redefining boundaries or prioritizing your spiritual well-being.

Listening to God's Direction

POSITIONING YOURSELF FOR GOD'S PLAN ALSO INVOLVES LEARNING to hear His voice. While God speaks in various ways—through Scripture, circumstances, and other people—the most intimate way to listen to Him is through the Holy Spirit.

Practical Ways to Listen

1. Spend Time in God's Word
    - The Bible is God's primary way of speaking to us. Regularly reading and meditating on Scripture equips you to discern His voice.
2. Be Still

- Psalm 46:10 says, "Be still, and know that I am God."*
  Cultivating stillness is key to hearing God's direction in a world of noise.
3. Seek Confirmation
    - When you believe God is speaking to you, seek confirmation through prayer, Scripture, and wise counsel from trusted spiritual mentors.

The Role of Obedience

Once you've positioned yourself to hear from God, the next step is obedience. Knowing God's plan is one thing, but following through requires 'faith and trust.'

Small Steps of Obedience:

Sometimes, God's plan unfolds gradually. Taking small steps of obedience in your daily life can lead to significant spiritual breakthroughs.

Trusting the Outcome:

Obedience often involves stepping out in faith without knowing the whole picture. Trust that God works all things together for your good (Romans 8:28).

Positioned for Purpose

Positioning yourself for God's plan is not a one-time event but a lifelong journey of surrender, growth, and alignment with His will. By clearing distractions, engaging in prayer and fasting, surrounding yourself with the right people, and listening for His direction, you create an environment where God can move powerfully.

As you take these steps, remember the promise of Jeremiah 29:11: God's plans for you are good and designed to give you hope and a future. Trust Him, position yourself, and watch as He unfolds His perfect plan in your life.

CHAPTER TWO
U – UNDERSTANDING YOUR IDENTITY IN CHRIST

KNOWING WHO YOU ARE IN GOD

Understanding your identity in Christ is the cornerstone of living a purposeful life and fulfilling God's divine plan. Without a firm grasp of who you are in Christ, it becomes easy to be swayed by the enemy's lies, the expectations of others, or the challenges of life. However, God's Word provides a clear and empowering picture of your true identity:

"BUT YOU ARE A CHOSEN PEOPLE, A ROYAL PRIESTHOOD, A HOLY NATION, God's special possession, that you may declare the praises of him who called you out of darkness into his wonderful light." 1 Peter 2:9

THIS CHAPTER EXPLORES THE SIGNIFICANCE OF BEING A CHILD OF God, intricately crafted and remarkable, and how grasping your identity can reveal your God-given potential. You will learn how your distinct gifts, talents, and experiences are intended to glorify God and make a difference in the world.

The Struggle to Understand Identity

THE QUESTION OF IDENTITY HAS BEEN A CENTRAL STRUGGLE FOR humanity since the beginning of time. In the Garden of Eden, the serpent challenged Eve's identity by planting seeds of doubt about her relationship with God:

"DID GOD SAY...?" GENESIS 3:1

THIS SAME TACTIC IS STILL USED BY THE ENEMY TODAY. HE SEEKS TO confuse and distort your understanding of who you are by whispering lies such as:

"You're not good enough."

"Your past defines you."

"You'll never measure up."

These falsehoods often stem from previous experiences, setbacks, or others' judgments. Yet, the reality is that these factors do not define who you are; your identity is shaped by what God declares about you.

You Are a Child of God

The most profound truth about your identity is that you are a child of God. This truth is echoed throughout Scripture:

"SEE WHAT GREAT LOVE THE FATHER HAS LAVISHED ON US, THAT WE should be called children of God! And that is what we are!" 1 John 3:1

What It Means to Be a Child of God

1. You Are Loved Unconditionally
   - God's love for you is not based on your performance or perfection. His love is constant and unwavering, rooted in His character, not your actions.
2. You Are Accepted
   - God welcomes you as His own in a world that often places conditions on acceptance. Through Jesus, you are entirely accepted into His family.
3. You Are Heir to God's Promises
   - As a child of God, you are an heir to all His promises. This includes His peace, provision, guidance, and eternal life.

Fearfully and Wonderfully Made

PSALM 139:14 DECLARES:

"I praise you because I am fearfully and wonderfully made; your works are wonderful, I know that full well."

Understanding this truth is essential to embracing your identity. You were created with intentionality, designed by a loving Creator who does not make mistakes.

God's Intentional Design

YOUR PERSONALITY

How you think, feel, and interact with the world is no accident. God gave you a unique personality to fulfill His purpose.

YOUR TALENTS AND GIFTS

Whether you are a natural leader, a creative artist, or a compassionate caregiver, your gifts are part of God's divine design.

YOUR PHYSICAL FEATURES

Even your appearance reflects God's creativity. You were designed to be exactly who you are.

BREAKING FREE FROM WORLDLY LABELS

Many people carry labels that don't align with their God-given identity. These labels may come from past mistakes, hurtful words, or societal pressures. However, these labels do not define you.

Steps to Break Free

1. IDENTIFY THE LIES
   - List the negative labels or beliefs you've accepted about yourself. Prayerfully ask God to reveal any lies you've been believing.
2. REPLACE LIES WITH TRUTH
   - Find Scriptures that counteract the lies. For example, if you feel unloved, meditate on Romans 8:38-39, which declares that nothing can separate you from God's love.
3. DECLARE GOD'S TRUTH OVER YOUR LIFE
   - Speak affirmations based on Scripture. For example, "I am a child of God" or "I am fearfully and wonderfully made."
4. SURROUND YOURSELF WITH ENCOURAGEMENT
   - Surround yourself with people who affirm your identity in Christ and help you grow in your faith.

EMBRACING YOUR SPIRITUAL GIFTS

Your identity in Christ includes the unique gifts and talents God has given you. These gifts reflect His creativity and are tools for fulfilling your purpose.

What Are Spiritual Gifts?

Spiritual gifts are abilities given by the Holy Spirit to believers to build up the Church and glorify God. Examples include teaching, hospitality, leadership, encouragement, and discernment 1 Corinthians 12:4-11.

How to Identify Your Gifts

1. PRAY FOR REVELATION
    - Ask God to reveal the gifts He has placed within you.
2. REFLECT ON YOUR PASSIONS
    - What are you naturally drawn to? Your passions often align with your spiritual gifts.
3. SEEK FEEDBACK
    - Ask trusted friends or mentors to share what they see as your strengths and gifts.
4. TRY NEW THINGS
    - Sometimes, discovering your gifts requires stepping out in faith and trying new roles or ministries.

Your Identity in the Body of Christ

AS A BELIEVER, YOU ARE A CHILD OF GOD AND A VITAL MEMBER OF the Body of Christ. Each member has a unique role to play:

"NOW YOU ARE THE BODY OF CHRIST, AND EACH OF YOU IS A PART OF IT."
1 Corinthians 12:27

Unity and Diversity

The Body of Christ is beautifully diverse. Your gifts, personality, and experiences contribute to the Church's overall mission. Embracing your identity means recognizing your role and valuing the roles of others.

Serving with Your Gifts

In the Church

Use your gifts to serve your local church community through teaching, worship, hospitality, or other ministries.

In the World

Your identity in Christ is not confined to the church building. Use your gifts to impact your workplace, neighborhood, and beyond.

Living Out Your Identity

Understanding your identity is the first step; living it out is where transformation happens. This requires daily surrender to God and a commitment to walking in His truth.

Practical Steps to Live Out Your Identity

1. RENEW YOUR MIND DAILY
    - Spend time in God's Word to remind yourself of who you are. Romans 12:2 encourages us to be transformed by the renewing of our minds.
2. WALK IN CONFIDENCE
    - Knowing who you are in Christ allows you to live confidently, free from fear and insecurity.
3. REFLECT CHRIST'S LOVE
    - Your identity is not just about who you are but who you reflect. Reflecting Christ's love for others is a natural outflow of understanding your identity.

Impacting the World Through Your Identity

YOUR IDENTITY IN CHRIST IS NOT JUST FOR YOUR BENEFIT, IT IS meant to impact the world. As 1 Peter 2:9 reminds us, we are called to declare God's praises and shine His light in a dark world.

Being Salt and Light

- Salt of the Earth

Salt preserves and adds flavor. Your presence should bring life, hope, and encouragement to those around you (Matthew 5:13).

- Light of the World

As a reflection of Christ, your life should illuminate the path to God for others (Matthew 5:14-16).

Making an Eternal Impact

Living out your identity makes you part of God's greater story. Whether you share the Gospel, serve others, or simply live faithfully, your life has eternal significance.

Embracing Who You Are

Understanding your identity in Christ is not about striving to become someone you're not; it's about embracing who God has already declared you to be. You are chosen, loved, and equipped for a unique purpose. By aligning your life with this truth, you can walk confidently in the freedom and power of knowing who you are in Christ.

As you continue this journey, remember the words of 1 Peter 2:9: You are God's special possession, called to declare His praises. Stand firm in your identity, live boldly in your purpose, and let your life shine as a testament to His glory.

PART TWO: RECOGNIZING AND PURSUING YOUR PURPOSE

R – RECOGNIZING YOUR CALLING

SIGNS OF YOUR GOD-GIVEN CALLING

God has a unique purpose for every individual. Your calling is how He desires you to serve Him and bring glory to His name. Recognizing this calling requires spiritual discernment, a heart open to His voice, and a willingness to step out in faith. Romans 8:28 reminds us of the assurance we have in God's plan:

"And we know that in all things God works for the good of those who love him, who have been called according to his purpose."

This chapter aims to help you understand the meaning of being called by God, how to recognize His guidance, and how your experiences—both triumphs and trials—align with His larger plan. Additionally, you will learn to identify divine opportunities and confidently embrace your purpose.

What Does It Mean to Be Called?

Being called by God is a divine invitation to participate in His mission. It is not reserved for pastors, missionaries, or church leaders; every believer is called to a life of purpose and service. Your calling reflects God's unique design for you, encompassing your gifts, passions, experiences, and the needs of the world around you.

General Calling vs. Specific Calling

1. General Calling
    - Every believer's general calling is to follow Christ, live a holy life, and make disciples (Matthew 28:19-20). This foundational calling shapes your identity and purpose.
2. Specific Calling
    - Your specific calling is the unique way God wants you to serve Him, whether in your career, ministry, family, or community. It often aligns with your spiritual gifts, passions, and life experiences.

RECOGNIZING GOD'S VOICE

The first step in recognizing your calling is discerning God's voice. God speaks in various ways—through Scripture, prayer, circumstances, and the counsel of others. However, hearing His voice requires intentionality and a heart attuned to His leading.

Ways God Speaks

1. THROUGH SCRIPTURE
    - The Bible is God's primary way of revealing His will. Regularly reading and meditating on Scripture allows you to understand His character and recognize His voice.
2. THROUGH PRAYER
    - Prayer is a two-way conversation with God. As you present your requests, take time to listen. He often places impressions, thoughts, or ideas on your heart.
3. THROUGH CIRCUMSTANCES
    - God leverages both positive and difficult experiences in your life to direct you toward your purpose. Notice the doors that open or close, and have faith in His sovereignty in all circumstances.

4. Through Wise Counsel
    - Trusted mentors, pastors, or spiritually mature friends can offer insights and help you discern God's leading. Proverbs 15:22 says, *"Plans fail for lack of counsel, but with many advisers they succeed."*
5. Through the Holy Spirit
    - The Holy Spirit prompts and guides believers in specific ways. Learn to recognize His nudges and trust His guidance.

Identifying Your Calling

Recognizing your calling often involves identifying the areas where God has uniquely equipped you to serve. This process includes evaluating your gifts, passions, and the needs around you.

STEP 1: DISCOVER YOUR SPIRITUAL GIFTS

Every believer is given spiritual gifts to serve the Body of Christ and glorify God. These gifts include teaching, leadership, mercy, discernment, encouragement, and more (1 Corinthians 12:4-11). Reflect on the following:

- What comes naturally to you?
- In what areas do others affirm your abilities?
- What activities bring you joy and fulfillment?

STEP 2: EXAMINE YOUR PASSIONS

God often aligns your calling with the things that stir your heart. Ask yourself:

- What burdens or injustices move me to action?
- What topics or causes ignite my enthusiasm?
- How can I use my passions to glorify God?

STEP 3: REFLECT ON YOUR LIFE EXPERIENCES

Your past experiences—both triumphs and trials—shape your calling. God never wastes a moment; even your pain has a purpose. Consider how your story can be a testimony to others and a tool for ministry.

STEP 4: LOOK FOR OPPORTUNITIES

Recognizing your calling involves being attentive to the opportunities God places before you. These could be ministry roles, career paths, or divine appointments with people in need. Stay open and flexible, trusting that God will guide your steps.

Recognizing Divine Opportunities

One key aspect of recognizing your calling is discerning divine opportunities. These are moments or situations where God invites you to step into His purpose. However, these opportunities often require faith and obedience.

Signs of a Divine Opportunity

1. IT ALIGNS WITH SCRIPTURE
    - A divine opportunity will never contradict God's Word. If it involves dishonesty, compromise, or sin, it is not from God.
2. IT REQUIRES FAITH
    - God often calls us to step out of our comfort zones. If an opportunity seems daunting but aligns with His will, it may be a sign of His leading.
3. IT GLORIFIES GOD
    - A divine opportunity will ultimately glorify God, not yourself. It will contribute to His kingdom and point others to Christ.
4. IT RESONATES WITH YOUR SPIRIT
    - The Holy Spirit often confirms divine opportunities by giving you peace or a sense of conviction about the decision.

Using Your Trials as Stepping Stones

Your trials and challenges are not obstacles to your calling but essential parts of the journey. God uses difficulties to refine you, grow your faith, and prepare you for His planned purpose.

Biblical Examples of Trials and Calling

1. JOSEPH
    - Trials marked Joseph's journey from slavery to leadership in Egypt, but each step prepared him for his ultimate purpose (Genesis 50:20).
2. MOSE
    - Moses spent 40 years in the wilderness before leading the Israelites out of Egypt. His waiting time was a period of preparation.
3. PAUL
    - Paul faced persecution, imprisonment, and suffering, yet he recognized these trials as opportunities to advance the Gospel (Philippians 1:12-14).

How to Use Your Trials

1. TRUST GOD'S SOVEREIGNTY
    - Believe that God is in control, even in challenging circumstances. He is working all things together for your good (Romans 8:28).
2. LEARN FROM THE EXPERIENCE
    - Every trial offers lessons that can strengthen your character and faith. Reflect on what God is teaching you through the process.
3. ENCOURAGE OTHERS
    - Your testimony of overcoming trials can inspire and uplift others facing similar struggles.

OVERCOMING BARRIERS TO RECOGNIZING YOUR CALLING

Certain barriers can prevent you from stepping into your purpose, even when God's calling is clear. These include fear, doubt, and a lack of trust in God's plan.

Barrier 1: Fear

Fear of failure, rejection, or the unknown can paralyze you. Remember:

- God has not given you a spirit of fear (2 Timothy 1:7).
- Trust that His strength will enable you to fulfill His calling.

Barrier 2: Doubt

Doubt often arises from feelings of inadequacy or comparison. Combat doubt by meditating on Scriptures that affirm your worth and abilities in Christ.

Barrier 3: Distractions

The enemy uses distractions to divert your focus from God's purpose. Clear distractions by prioritizing your time with God and aligning your actions with His will.

Living Out Your Calling

Recognizing your calling is just the beginning. Living it out requires faith, obedience, and perseverance. As you pursue your purpose, rely on God's strength and trust His timing.

Practical Steps to Live Out Your Calling

1. **Pray for Guidance**
    - Continually seek God's wisdom and direction in your journey.
2. **Take Action**

- Don't wait for the perfect moment. Step out in faith and trust that God will equip you.
3. STAY CONNECTED TO GOD
    - Abide in Christ through prayer, worship, and Scripture. Your relationship with Him is the foundation of your calling.
4. BE OPEN TO GROWTH
    - Your calling may evolve. Stay flexible and willing to adapt as God leads you.

Embrace the Call

Recognizing your calling is a journey of faith and discovery. It involves listening to God's voice, identifying your gifts, and stepping into divine opportunities with courage and trust. Remember that your trials are not setbacks but stepping stones toward your destiny.

As you walk in your calling, hold onto the promise of Romans 8:28: God is working all things together for your good and His glory. Embrace His unique purpose for you, and trust that He will equip and empower you every step of the way.

CHAPTER FOUR

P – PURSUING PURPOSE WITH PASSION

FINDING PASSION IN YOUR WORK

Once you recognize your calling, the next step is to actively pursue it with passion and determination. God designed your purpose not as a distant goal but as a living reality fueled by enthusiasm and commitment. Passion is the driving force behind your purpose, providing the energy and perseverance needed to overcome challenges. Colossians 3:23 reminds us of the attitude we must bring to our work:

"Whatever you do, work at it with all your heart, as working for the Lord, not for human masters."

THIS CHAPTER EXPLORES WHAT IT MEANS TO PURSUE YOUR GOD-given purpose with passion, how to overcome obstacles like fear and procrastination, and practical steps to stay committed to your goals while trusting God in every season.

The Importance of Passion in Pursuing Purpose

Passion is the emotional energy that propels you forward in your purpose. It breathes life into your calling, ignites creativity, and sustains you through difficulties. Without passion, even the most significant purpose can feel like a burden rather than a blessing.

Why Passion Matters

1. It Reflects God's Design
   - God created you with specific passions and interests that align with the purpose He has placed in your heart.
2. It Fuels Perseverance
   - Passion helps you push through challenges and setbacks, reminding you of the "why" behind your efforts.
3. It Inspires Others
   - When you pursue your purpose with passion, your enthusiasm motivates and encourages others to do the same.

How Passion and Purpose Connect

Purpose without passion becomes a duty, and passion without purpose becomes aimless energy. When the two come together, they create a powerful force that drives meaningful impact. Your passion is a gift from God, meant to energize and direct your pursuit of His calling.

OVERCOMING FEAR AND PROCRASTINATION

While pursuing your purpose is exciting, fear and procrastination are two significant obstacles that can hold you back. Both are rooted in doubt, doubt in yourself, your abilities, or even God's plan. Recognizing and addressing these barriers is essential to moving forward.

Confronting Fear

Fear frequently masquerades as practicality or caution. It whispers deceitful messages like, "You're not good enough," "You will fail," or "It's too risky." If left unaddressed, these fears can immobilize you.

1. **IDENTIFY THE ROOT OF FEAR**
   - Ask yourself: What am I afraid of? Failure? Rejection? Uncertainty? Naming the fear takes away some of its power.
2. **COMBAT FEAR WITH FAITH**
   - Replace fear with trust in God's promises. Meditate on Scriptures such as Isaiah 41:10: *"Do not fear, for I am with you; do not be dismayed, for I am your God."*
3. **TAKE SMALL STEPS OF OBEDIENCE**
   - Courage doesn't mean the absence of fear; it means taking action despite it. Start small and trust God to guide you at each step.

Overcoming Procrastination

Procrastination frequently arises from perfectionism or feeling overwhelmed. It can hinder your progress and take away the joy of chasing your purpose.

1. **BREAK TASKS INTO MANAGEABLE STEPS**
   - Significant goals can feel daunting. Divide them into smaller, actionable steps to make progress feel achievable.
2. **SET DEADLINES AND ACCOUNTABILITY**
   - Establish realistic deadlines and share your goals with someone who can hold you accountable.
3. **FOCUS ON PROGRESS, NOT PERFECTION**
   - God doesn't expect perfection; He desires faithfulness. Celebrate small wins and trust Him with the results.

Practical Steps to Pursue Purpose with Passion

Passion alone is not enough; it must be paired with action. Below are practical steps to help you stay committed to your purpose and work toward your goals with determination and enthusiasm.

STEP 1: SET CLEAR GOALS

A clear vision of what you want to achieve provides direction and motivation. Your goals should align with your calling and reflect God's priorities for your life.

1. PRAY FOR GUIDANCE
    - Seek God's wisdom as you set your goals. Ask Him to reveal what He wants you to focus on.
2. WRITE DOWN YOUR GOALS
    - Writing your goals makes them tangible and helps you stay accountable.
3. ALIGN YOUR GOALS WITH SCRIPTURE
    - Ensure your goals are consistent with biblical principles and bring glory to God.

STEP 2: DEVELOP A PLAN

A goal without a plan is just a wish. Break your goals into actionable steps and create a roadmap for achieving them.

1. CREATE A TIMELINE
    - Set specific deadlines for each step to stay on track.
2. PRIORITIZE YOUR TASKS
    - Focus on what is most important and avoid getting sidetracked by less significant activities.
3. STAY FLEXIBLE
    - Be willing to adjust your plan as God leads. Trust His timing over your own.

STEP 3: CULTIVATE DAILY DISCIPLINE

Passion may ignite the journey, but discipline sustains it. Developing consistent habits and routines helps you stay committed to your purpose.

1. START YOUR DAY WITH GOD
    - Spend time in prayer and Scripture to center your heart and mind on Him.

2. SET ASIDE TIME FOR YOUR GOALS
   - Dedicate specific blocks each day or week to work on your purpose.
3. ELIMINATE DISTRACTIONS
   - Identify what distracts you and take steps to minimize or remove it from your environment.

STEP 4: CELEBRATE PROGRESS

Acknowledging your achievements, no matter how small, keeps you motivated and focused on the bigger picture.

1. REFLECT ON GOD'S FAITHFULNESS
   - Take time to thank God for your progress and the opportunities He's provided.
2. REWARD YOURSELF
   - Celebrate milestones with meaningful rewards that encourage you to keep going.
3. SHARE YOUR SUCCESS
   - Share your progress with trusted friends or mentors who can rejoice with you and offer encouragement.

TRUSTING GOD IN EVERY SEASON

Pursuing your purpose is not a linear journey. There will be seasons of growth, waiting, and even setbacks. Trusting God in every season is essential to staying faithful to your calling.

SEASON OF PREPARATION

Sometimes, God places you in a season of preparation before allowing you to step fully into your purpose.

EMBRACE THE PROCESS

Trust that God is working in you during this time, even if you don't see immediate results.

Focus on Growth

Use this season to develop your gifts, deepen your relationship with God, and serve where you are.

Season of Action

In seasons of action, God provides opportunities to pursue your purpose actively.

Stay Focused

Avoid becoming distracted by secondary goals or activities.

Give Your Best Effort

Work wholeheartedly, as Colossians 3:23 encourages, knowing your efforts are for the Lord.

Season of Waiting

Waiting is one of the most challenging seasons, but it is often where God does His most remarkable work in your heart.

Trust God's Timing

Believe that His timing is perfect, even when it doesn't match your expectations.

Stay Faithful

Continue to pray, serve, and prepare, trusting that God is working behind the scenes.

Overcoming Discouragement

Discouragement is inevitable when pursuing your purpose, but it doesn't have to derail you. Learning to handle setbacks and challenges gracefully is vital to staying passionate.

1. REMEMBER GOD'S PROMISES
    - When discouragement sets in, cling to God's Word. Promises such as Isaiah 40:31—*"But those who hope in the Lord will renew their strength"*—offer hope and encouragement.
2. SEEK COMMUNITY
    - Surround yourself with people who will encourage and pray for you. Sharing your struggles with trusted friends or mentors can lighten the burden.
3. REFOCUS ON YOUR WHY
    - When you lose motivation, revisit the reason behind your purpose. Remind yourself of the impact your calling has on others and the glory it brings to God.

Living Out Your Purpose for God's Glory

Ultimately, pursuing your purpose with passion is about glorifying God. It's not about personal success or recognition but about using your gifts and talents to honor Him and make a difference in the world.

Keep an Eternal Perspective

Remember that your purpose has eternal significance. Your work for God will have a lasting impact beyond this life.

Rely on God's Strength

Pursuing purpose with passion is not about striving in your strength. Philippians 4:13 reminds us: *"I can do all this through him who gives me strength."*

Pursue with Passion

Pursuing your God-given purpose is a journey of faith, determination, and joy. By overcoming fear and procrastination, setting clear goals, cultivating daily discipline, and trusting God in every season, you can pursue your calling passionately and make a lasting impact.

Remember the truth of Colossians 3:23: Work at your purpose with all your heart, knowing that you are serving the Lord. Let your passion for God and His plans fuel your journey, and trust that He will guide you every step of the way.

PART THREE: LIVING OUT YOUR PURPOSE
O – OVERCOMING OBSTACLES WITH FAITH

Living out your God-given purpose does not guarantee a life free from challenges. In fact, fulfilling your calling often involves facing trials, opposition, and setbacks. However, obstacles are not meant to derail your purpose—they are opportunities for growth and deeper reliance on God. Through faith, you can overcome any challenge, as Philippians 4:13 reminds us:

"I can do all things through Christ who strengthens me."

THIS CHAPTER WILL HELP YOU SUSTAIN FAITH IN TOUGH TIMES, cultivate spiritual resilience, and view hardships as elements of God's refining process. These concepts will assist you in tackling life's challenges with assurance and determination.

Understanding the Purpose of Obstacles

Obstacles are a natural part of life and often play a significant role in shaping your character and strengthening your faith. While they may seem like interruptions to your plans, they are integral to God's purpose for your life.

Why God Allows Obstacles

1. TO REFINE YOUR CHARACTER
   - Just as gold is refined through fire, God uses challenges to purify your heart, develop humility, and deepen your trust in Him (1 Peter 1:6-7).
2. TO STRENGTHEN YOUR FAITH
   - Trials push you to rely on God rather than your own strength. They remind you of your dependence on Him and build endurance (James 1:2-4).
3. TO PREPARE YOU FOR GREATER PURPOSE:
   - Obstacles are often training grounds for what lies ahead. They teach perseverance, equip you with wisdom, and prepare you for the next level of your calling.
4. TO GLORIFY GOD
   - Overcoming challenges through faith is a testimony of God's power and faithfulness. Your victory can inspire and encourage others to trust Him.

DEVELOPING SPIRITUAL RESILIENCE

Spiritual resilience is the ability to endure hardships while maintaining faith and hope in God. It is not the absence of struggles but the strength to persevere through them. Developing resilience equips you to face life's challenges with confidence and grace.

Keys to Building Resilience

1. ANCHOR YOURSELF IN GOD'S WORD
   - Scripture is your greatest source of encouragement and guidance during trials. Meditate on promises like Isaiah 41:10: *"So do not fear, for I am with you; do not be dismayed, for I am your God."*
2. CULTIVATE A STRONG PRAYER LIFE
   - Prayer connects you to God's strength and peace. Be honest with Him about your struggles, and ask for the wisdom and endurance to navigate them.

3. FOCUS ON GOD'S FAITHFULNESS
   - Reflect on your past triumphs and how God has supported you during tough times. Recalling His unwavering faithfulness strengthens your faith in facing present and upcoming challenges.
4. SURROUND YOURSELF WITH SUPPORT
   - Resilience is strengthened in community. Seek encouragement and accountability from fellow believers who can pray for you and offer wise counsel.

Maintaining Faith in Adversity

Faith serves as the cornerstone for navigating obstacles. Your outlook and reactions can significantly impact how you confront challenges. Upholding faith demands intentionality and a focus on God's promises instead of your situations.

Faith Over Fear

Fear is one of the enemy's primary weapons during difficult times. It can paralyze you and make obstacles seem insurmountable. Combat fear with faith by:

1. DECLARING GOD'S PROMISES
   - Speak Scriptures like 2 Timothy 1:7 over your life: *"For the Spirit God gave us does not make us timid, but gives us power, love, and self-discipline."*
2. CHOOSING TRUST
   - Faith is a choice to trust God, even when the outcome is uncertain. Remind yourself that He is in control and working for your good (Romans 8:28).

Faith in God's Timing

Waiting on God's timing can be one of the most challenging aspects of faith. Delays often feel like obstacles, but they are opportunities to grow in patience and trust.

1. SURRENDER YOUR TIMELINE
    - Release your need for control and trust that God's timing is perfect. His delays are not denials but preparations.
2. SEEK GOD'S WILL
    - Use seasons of waiting to align your desires with God's plan. Ask Him to reveal what He wants you to learn or focus on during this time.

Reframing Your Struggles

A critical aspect of overcoming obstacles is shifting your perspective. Instead of viewing challenges as barriers, see them as opportunities for growth and refinement. This mindset allows you to face difficulties with hope and resilience.

Obstacles as Opportunities

1. OPPORTUNITIES FOR GROWTH
    - Struggles often reveal areas where you need to grow, whether in patience, humility, or dependence on God. Embrace the refining process as part of your journey.
2. OPPORTUNITIES FOR MINISTRY
    - Your struggles can become a powerful testimony to others. Sharing how God helped you overcome challenges can inspire and uplift those facing similar battles.
3. OPPORTUNITIES TO DEEPEN YOUR FAITH
    - Adversity forces you to rely on God in ways you may not during easier times. It strengthens your relationship with Him and deepens your trust.

God's Perspective on Struggles

Romans 5:3-5 offers a profound perspective on hardships:

"Not only so, but we also glory in our sufferings because we know that suffering produces perseverance; perseverance, character; and character, hope."

This passage reminds us that God uses struggles to develop essential qualities in us so that He can fulfill His purpose.

Practical Steps to Overcome Obstacles

While spiritual resilience and faith are foundational, there are also practical steps to effectively navigate challenges.

1. ACKNOWLEDGE THE OBSTACLE
    - Ignoring or denying a challenge doesn't make it go away. Be honest about the situation and bring it before God in prayer. Admit your need for His guidance and strength.
2. SEEK GOD'S PERSPECTIVE
    - Ask God to show you His perspective on the obstacle. What is He teaching you through this situation? How can you grow from it? This shift in mindset can transform your approach.
3. TAKE ACTION IN FAITH
    - Overcoming obstacles often requires action. Trust God to guide your steps and give you the courage to move forward, even when the path is unclear.
4. LEAN ON YOUR SUPPORT SYSTEM
    - You were never meant to face challenges alone. Share your struggles with trusted friends, family, or mentors who can pray for you, offer advice, and encourage you.
5. STAY FOCUSED ON YOUR PURPOSE
    - Obstacles can distract you from your calling. Remind yourself of your purpose and stay committed to pursuing it, even in the face of difficulties.

EXAMPLES OF OVERCOMING OBSTACLES IN SCRIPTURE

The Bible is filled with stories of individuals who faced incredible challenges but overcame them through faith. Their examples serve as inspiration and encouragement for us today.

JOSEPH: FROM PRISON TO PALACE

Betrayal, false accusations, and imprisonment marked Joseph's journey. Despite these obstacles, he remained faithful to God and eventually rose to a position of significant influence in Egypt. Joseph's story reminds us that God's plans are greater than our circumstances (Genesis 50:20).

Moses: Leading Through Opposition

Moses faced numerous challenges, including Pharaoh's resistance, the Israelites' complaints, and his own insecurities. He relied on God's strength and guidance through each obstacle to lead His people to freedom (Exodus 14:13-14).

Paul: Persevering in Persecution

The Apostle Paul endured imprisonment, beatings, and constant opposition, yet he remained steadfast in his mission to spread the Gospel. His letters are a testament to the power of faith in overcoming trials (Philippians 4:11-13).

The Refining Process

One of the most powerful truths about obstacles is that they are part of God's refining process. Just as a craftsman refines silver by exposing it to fire, God uses trials to purify and strengthen your faith.

What Refining Looks Like

1. Removing Impurities
   - Challenges reveal areas in your life that need surrender, whether pride, fear, or self-reliance.
2. Strengthening Your Faith
   - The refining process deepens your trust in God and equips you to handle greater responsibilities.
3. Preparing You for Impact
   - God uses the lessons learned during trials to prepare you for greater purpose and influence.

FAITH OVERCOMES ALL

Overcoming obstacles with faith is not about avoiding challenges but facing them with courage and trust in God. By developing spiritual resilience, reframing your struggles, and relying on God's strength, you can navigate life's difficulties with confidence and hope.

Remember Philippians 4:13: *"You can do all things through Christ who strengthens you."* Embrace your obstacles as opportunities for growth and refining, trusting that God is using them to prepare you for your greater purpose. Through faith, you can overcome anything and live out His calling on your life.

CHAPTER SIX

S – STEPPING OUT IN BOLDNESS

CONFRONTING FEAR AND INSECURITIES

Walking in your God-given purpose requires boldness—a courageous willingness to trust God, step out of your comfort zone, and take risks for His glory. Boldness is not the absence of fear but the presence of faith that enables you to act despite it. Proverbs 28:1 offers a powerful reminder of the confidence we have in God:

"The righteous are as bold as a lion."

THIS CHAPTER WILL EMPOWER YOU TO CONFRONT FEAR AND DOUBT head-on and take courageous steps toward your destiny. You will learn to draw strength from God, overcome the barriers that hold you back, and lead others by example through your bold faith and actions.

What Does It Mean to Step Out in Boldness?

Boldness is more than just confidence; it is a spiritual courage that comes from knowing who God is and who you are in Him. It's rooted in faith and fueled by the understanding that God is with you and working through you.

Characteristics of Boldness in Christ

1. **FAITH OVER FEAR**
   - Boldness is choosing faith over fear, trusting God's power and promises even when the path ahead is uncertain.
2. **OBEDIENCE WITHOUT HESITATION**
   - Boldness requires immediate and wholehearted obedience to God's instructions, regardless of personal doubts or the opinions of others.
3. **A WILLINGNESS TO TAKE RISKS**
   - Boldness often involves stepping into the unknown or taking actions that seem risky from a worldly perspective, knowing that God will provide and protect.
4. **CONFIDENCE IN GOD'S STRENGTH**
   - True boldness is not about self-reliance but leaning on God's strength and wisdom.

THE BIBLICAL CALL TO BOLDNESS

Throughout Scripture, God calls His people to step out boldly for His purposes. These examples inspire and remind us that boldness is part of walking in faith.

JOSHUA: LEADING WITH COURAGE

When Joshua succeeded Moses as the leader of Israel, he faced the daunting task of leading the people into the Promised Land. God encouraged him with these words:

"Have I not commanded you? Be strong and courageous. Do not be afraid; do not be discouraged, for the Lord your God will be with you wherever you go." Joshua 1:9

Joshua's story teaches us that boldness begins with trusting God's promises and presence.

ESTHER: RISKING EVERYTHING FOR A GREATER PURPOSE

Queen Esther displayed extraordinary boldness when she approached King Xerxes to save her people, knowing it could cost her life. Her famous words, *"If I perish, I perish."* (Esther 4:16), reflect the kind of faith-driven courage God calls us to have.

PETER AND JOHN: BOLD WITNESSES

Peter and John boldly proclaimed the Gospel in the New Testament despite threats and persecution. Their response to the opposition was rooted in their faith:

"We cannot help speaking about what we have seen and heard." Acts 4:20

Their example reminds us that boldness often involves standing firm in our convictions and sharing our faith, even when it's unpopular or dangerous.

CONFRONTING FEAR AND DOUBT

Fear and doubt are two of the most significant barriers to boldness. They can paralyze you, keeping you from stepping into your purpose and fulfilling God's call on your life. Overcoming these barriers requires intentional effort and reliance on God.

Overcoming Fear

1. ACKNOWLEDGE YOUR FEAR
   - Pretending fear doesn't exist will not make it go away. Be honest with God about what scares you, and ask Him for the courage to face it.
2. REPLACE FEAR WITH TRUTH
   - Fear thrives on lies. Combat it by meditating on Scriptures that affirm God's protection and provision, such as Isaiah 41:10: *"So do not fear, for I am with you; do not be dismayed, for I am your God."*
3. TAKE SMALL STEPS OF FAITH

- Boldness is built one step at a time. Start by taking small actions of obedience and watch as your confidence in God grows.

Conquering Doubt

1. **TRUST GOD'S CHARACTER**
   - Doubt often stems from uncertainty about God's plan or goodness. Remind yourself of His faithfulness and trustworthiness.
2. **SEEK CLARITY THROUGH PRAYER**
   - When doubt clouds your vision, ask God for wisdom and direction. James 1:5 promises that He gives wisdom generously to those who ask.
3. **SURROUND YOURSELF WITH ENCOURAGEMENT**
   - Surround yourself with people who will speak life and truth into your situation. Their support can help dispel doubt and renew your confidence.

PRACTICAL STEPS TO STEP OUT IN BOLDNESS

Boldness is not a one-time decision but a daily practice. Below are practical steps to help you cultivate boldness and walk confidently in your purpose.

STEP 1: KNOW YOUR IDENTITY IN CHRIST

Boldness begins with understanding who you are in Christ. When you know that you are chosen, loved, and empowered by God, you can confidently face any challenge.

1. **MEDITATE ON SCRIPTURE**
   - Study verses like 2 Timothy 1:7: *"For the Spirit God gave us does not make us timid, but gives us power, love, and self-discipline."*
2. **DECLARE YOUR IDENTITY**
   - Speak affirmations based on God's Word, such as *"I am a child of God"* and *"I am equipped for every good work."*

3. REJECT LIES
    - Identify and reject thoughts or beliefs that contradict what God says about you.

STEP 2: TRUST GOD'S PROMISES

God's promises are the foundation of boldness. When you trust His Word, you can step out in faith, knowing He will fulfill what He has spoken.

1. MEMORIZE KEY PROMISES
    - Memorize verses that strengthen your faith, such as Jeremiah 29:11: *"For I know the plans I have for you... plans to give you hope and a future."*
2. APPLY HIS PROMISES
    - Use God's promises as a guide for your decisions. For example, if He promises to provide, take steps of faith in areas that require provision.
3. REMIND YOURSELF OFTEN
    - Regularly remind yourself of God's faithfulness by reflecting on past experiences where He came through for you.

STEP 3: TAKE ACTION DESPITE UNCERTAINTY

Boldness requires stepping out even when the outcome is unclear. Trust that God will guide and equip you as you go.

1. START SMALL
    - Begin with manageable steps of faith. Each step builds confidence and prepares you for more significant challenges.
2. EMBRACE THE UNKNOWN
    - Accept that you won't have all the answers. Walking by faith means trusting God with the details.
3. LEARN FROM FAILURE
    - Don't let fear of failure hold you back. Failure is often a stepping stone to growth and success.

Bold Leadership: Leading by Example

Boldness is not just for your journey; it's also a powerful tool for influencing and inspiring others. When you boldly lead, you set an example for others to follow.

What Bold Leadership Looks Like

1. COURAGEOUS DECISION-MAKING
   - Bold leaders make decisions rooted in faith, not fear. They trust God's wisdom and act with confidence.
2. AUTHENTICITY
   - Bold leaders are honest about their struggles and victories, showing others that courage is a journey, not a destination.
3. ENCOURAGING OTHERS
   - Bold leaders uplift and empower those around them, helping others confidently step into their own purpose.

How to Lead Boldly

1. MODEL FAITH IN ACTION:
   - Let your actions reflect your trust in God. Whether you share your faith, pursue a vision, or take a risk, your example can inspire others.
2. ENCOURAGE BOLDNESS IN OTHERS
   - Encourage those around you to take steps of faith. Offer support, prayer, and affirmation as they pursue their callings.
3. STAY HUMBLE
   - Remember that your boldness is rooted in God's strength, not your own. Give Him the glory for every victory.

Boldness in Everyday Life

Boldness is not just for big decisions or dramatic moments; it's also about living courageously in the everyday. Whether it's sharing your faith, standing up for what's right, or pursuing a personal goal, boldness is a daily choice.

BOLDNESS IN RELATIONSHIPS

1. SPEAK TRUTH IN LOVE
   - Be willing to have honest conversations, even when it's uncomfortable.
2. EXTEND FORGIVENESS
   - Boldness includes letting go of grudges and offering grace to others.
3. SHARE YOUR FAITH
   - Share the Gospel with others, trusting God to use your words.

BOLDNESS IN YOUR WORK

1. EXCEL IN EXCELLENCE
   - Approach your work with integrity and diligence, knowing you serve God (Colossians 3:23).
2. TAKE RISKS FOR GROWTH:
   - Pursue opportunities that challenge you and align with God's purpose for your life.
3. BE A LIGHT:
   - Let your boldness reflect Christ in your workplace, inspiring others through your actions and attitude.

WALK BOLDLY INTO YOUR DESTINY

Stepping out in boldness is essential for fulfilling your God-given purpose. It requires faith, courage, and a willingness to trust God in every step. Remember the truth of Proverbs 28:1: *"The righteous are as bold as a lion."* With God on your side, you can confront fear, overcome doubt, and take courageous steps toward your destiny.

CHAPTER SEVEN
E— EMBRACING YOUR ETERNAL IMPACT

LIVING FOR LEGACY, NOT JUST SUCCESS

Living with purpose transcends personal success or the fulfillment of individual dreams. It's about recognizing and embracing the eternal impact of your life. Every step taken in alignment with God's plan contributes to something far greater than yourself: the advancement of His Kingdom and the transformation of the world through His love.

Matthew 5:16 reminds us of the importance of living with purpose:

"Let your light shine before others, that they may see your good deeds and glorify your Father in heaven."

THIS CHAPTER WILL HELP YOU GRASP HOW TO APPROACH EACH DAY with an everlasting perspective, acknowledging that your life contributes to a greater divine narrative. You'll discover ways to create a legacy of faith, love, and hope that resonates with others well beyond your time.

The Eternal Perspective

An eternal perspective involves recognizing the fleeting nature of life's worries and concentrating on what is truly significant—your relationship with God, your influence on others, and the realization of His Kingdom's objectives.

Why Your Eternal Impact Matters

1. **Your Life Reflects God's Glory**
   - You were created to glorify God in everything you do. Living with an eternal perspective ensures that your life points others to Him.
2. **Your Actions Have Lasting Significance**
   - What you do today affects not only your future but also the lives of others for generations to come. Every act of faith, love, and obedience carries eternal consequences.
3. **You Are Part of God's Greater Plan**
   - God's plan for your life is intricately woven into His story of redemption and restoration. Embracing your eternal impact allows you to participate in this divine mission.

Living for God's Glory

Your ultimate purpose is to glorify God. When your actions, words, and decisions align with His will, you become a beacon of hope and love in a world that desperately needs Him.

How to Glorify God in Your Daily Life

1. **Live with Integrity**
   - Your character is a powerful witness to God's goodness. Strive to live in a way that honors Him, even when no one is watching.
2. **Reflect Christ's Love**
   - Demonstrate God's love through your words and actions. Whether it's showing kindness to a stranger or forgiving

someone who wronged you, your compassion reflects His heart.
3. **USE YOUR GIFTS FOR HIS KINGDOM:**
    - Your talents and abilities are not just for personal gain. Use them to serve others and advance God's mission in the world.
4. **SHARE THE GOSPEL**
    - One of the most impactful ways to glorify God is by sharing the message of salvation with others. Your testimony can lead others to experience His grace and love.

LEAVING A LEGACY OF FAITH AND LOVE

Living purposefully means leaving a legacy that outlives you—a legacy of faith, love, and service that impacts future generations. This legacy is not about fame or recognition but about faithfully fulfilling God's call on your life.

WHAT IS A LEGACY OF FAITH?

1. **A LIFE ROOTED IN GOD'S WORD**
    - A legacy of faith begins with a deep commitment to God's Word and living according to His principles.
2. **A LIFE OF INFLUENCE**
    - Your words and actions have the power to inspire others to seek God and live for Him.
3. **A LIFE OF SERVICE**
    - Serving others with humility and love leaves a lasting impact that reflects Christ's heart.

HOW TO BUILD YOUR LEGACY

1. **INVEST IN RELATIONSHIPS**
    - Your eternal impact is often most evident in the lives you touch. Prioritize meaningful relationships with your family, friends, and community.

2. MENTOR THE NEXT GENERATION
   - Share your wisdom, experiences, and faith with younger generations. Encourage them to pursue their God-given purpose.
3. SERVE SACRIFICIALLY
   - Look for opportunities to give your time, resources, and talents to those in need. Your acts of service demonstrate God's love and leave a lasting imprint.
4. STAY FAITHFUL TO THE END
   - A lasting legacy is built through consistent faithfulness over time. Persevere in your walk with God and trust Him to use your life for His glory.

Living Each Day with Eternal Significance

Living with an eternal perspective means approaching each day as an opportunity to make a difference in God's Kingdom. This mindset transforms ordinary moments into opportunities for impact.

STEPS TO EMBRACE ETERNAL SIGNIFICANCE

1. PRAY FOR GUIDANCE
   - Begin each day by asking God to guide your steps and show you how to make an eternal impact.
2. PRIORITIZE WHAT MATTERS
   - Focus on activities and decisions that align with God's will. Avoid distractions that pull you away from your purpose.
3. PRACTICE GRATITUDE
   - A thankful heart keeps you focused on God's blessings and reminds you of His faithfulness.
4. LOOK FOR DIVINE APPOINTMENTS
   - Be attentive to the opportunities God gives you to encourage, serve, or share His love with others.

Overcoming Barriers to Eternal Impact

While living with an eternal perspective is vital, it's not always easy. Barriers such as busyness, discouragement, and fear can hinder your ability to focus on what truly matters.

Barrier 1: Busyness

In a fast-paced world, it's easy to get caught up in the demands of daily life and lose sight of your eternal purpose.

Solution:

Simplify your schedule by prioritizing God's will. Say no to activities that don't align with your purpose, and make time for what matters most.

Barrier 2: Discouragement

When challenges arise, it's natural to feel discouraged. However, discouragement can cause you to lose sight of your impact and purpose.

Solution:

Reflect on God's promises and trust His plan. Surround yourself with a supportive community, and remember that your struggles are part of His refining process.

Barrier 3: Fear

Fear of failure or rejection can prevent you from stepping out in faith and pursuing your purpose.

Solution:

Replace fear with faith by meditating on Scriptures like 2 Timothy 1:7:

"For the Spirit God gave us does not make us timid, but gives us power, love, and self-discipline."

Examples of Eternal Impact in Scripture

The Bible is filled with stories of individuals whose lives had eternal significance. Their faith, obedience, and willingness to embrace their purpose offer valuable lessons for us today.

ABRAHAM: THE FATHER OF NATIONS

Abraham's faith and obedience to God laid the foundation for a covenant that impacts all believers. His legacy reminds us that even small steps of faith can have eternal consequences.

RUTH: A LEGACY OF LOYALTY

Ruth's loyalty and faithfulness not only changed her life but also played a role in God's plan of redemption through Jesus's lineage. Her story shows that everyday acts of faith can have far-reaching impact.

PAUL: A LIFE OF PURPOSE

The Apostle Paul dedicated his life to spreading the Gospel, often facing persecution and hardship. His letters continue to encourage and guide believers worldwide, proving that a life lived for God leaves an eternal mark.

ETERNAL IMPACT IN YOUR SPHERE OF INFLUENCE

You don't have to be a missionary or pastor to have an eternal impact. God has placed you in your unique sphere of influence—your family, workplace, community, and beyond—to shine His light and make a difference.

IN YOUR FAMILY

- BE INTENTIONAL ABOUT SHARING YOUR FAITH WITH YOUR CHILDREN AND LOVED ONES.
- MODEL CHRIST-LIKE BEHAVIOR AND VALUES.
- PRAY FOR AND WITH YOUR FAMILY, TRUSTING GOD TO WORK IN THEIR LIVES.
- IN YOUR WORKPLACE
  - Approach your work with excellence, knowing it reflects God's character.

- Look for opportunities to encourage and uplift your coworkers.
- Share your faith through your actions and conversations.
- IN YOUR COMMUNITY
  - Serve your neighbors and look for ways to meet their needs.
  - Get involved in ministries or organizations that align with your purpose.
  - Be a source of hope and love to those around you.

THE ETERNAL REWARD

Living with an eternal perspective not only impacts others but also deepens your relationship with God and prepares you for your ultimate reward. Colossians 3:23-24 reminds us:

"Whatever you do, work at it with all your heart, as working for the Lord, not for human masters, since you know that you will receive an inheritance from the Lord as a reward."

Your faithfulness in living out your purpose will be rewarded in eternity, and the lives you touch will be part of the legacy you bring before God.

SHINE BRIGHT FOR ETERNITY

Embracing your eternal impact means living each day with purpose, passion, and a focus on God's Kingdom. Your life is not just about the here and now; it's about fulfilling God's plan to bring hope, love, and transformation to the world.

As Matthew 5:16 encourages, let your light shine before others so they may see your good deeds and glorify your Father in heaven. Live boldly, love deeply, and pursue your purpose with the confidence that your life has eternal significance. Your impact today will ripple through eternity, bringing glory to God and hope to countless lives.

LIVING A LIFE OF WORTH

When you walk in your **P.U.R.P.O.S.E.**, you align yourself with God's perfect will, stepping into the life He has uniquely designed for you. Your worth is not defined by worldly standards, achievements, or the opinions of others—it is rooted in your identity as a child of God, fearfully and wonderfully made. As you embrace this truth, you begin to live with passion, strength, and resilience, knowing who you are in Christ and fulfilling His eternal calling.

The Apostle Paul's words in Ephesians 3:20-21 remind us of the incredible power of God working within us:

"Now to him who is able to do immeasurably more than all we ask or imagine, according to his power that is at work within us, to him be glory in the church and in Christ Jesus throughout all generations, forever and ever! Amen."

This journey of purpose is not one you undertake alone. God's power, working in and through you, enables you to overcome obstacles, walk in boldness, and leave an eternal impact. As you reflect on the lessons within this book, consider how you can live a life of worth—one that glorifies God and transforms the world around you.

LIVING YOUR PURPOSE, KNOWING YOUR WORTH

Walking in your purpose is more than a series of steps—it is a lifelong commitment to align your heart and life with God's will. It's about recognizing these truths:

1. **YOU ARE CHOSEN**
   - God has called you by name. You are not here by accident; you are here on purpose, for a purpose.
2. **YOU ARE EMPOWERED**
   - You have everything you need through the Holy Spirit to fulfill your calling. God's power is at work in you, equipping you for every good work.
3. **YOU ARE LOVED**
   - Your worth is not based on what you do but on who you are in Christ. Your Creator loves you unconditionally.

As you move forward, let your life reflect God's glory. Step out in faith, take bold actions, and trust that God can do "immeasurably more" than you could ever imagine.

A CALL TO RISE

Now is the time to rise. The world needs your light, your gifts, and your testimony. As you live out your purpose, you will inspire others to do the same. Your journey will not always be easy—there will be challenges, doubts, and moments of uncertainty—but remember this:

- **GOD IS WITH YOU:** He will never leave or forsake you.
- **YOUR IMPACT IS ETERNAL:** What you do for the Kingdom of God will have a lasting legacy.
- **YOUR WORTH IS SECURE:** No one can take away the identity and purpose God has given you.

Rise each day with the determination to make a difference, to love others well, and to glorify God in all you do.

For Those Who Are Unsure of Their Worth

Perhaps as you've read this book, you've felt a tug on your heart, but you're unsure of your relationship with God. Maybe you've struggled to see your worth, wondering if you truly have a purpose or if God could ever use you. Let me assure you: God loves you deeply and has a plan for your life.

The initial step to a fulfilling life begins with forming a relationship with Jesus Christ. Through Him, we find salvation, forgiveness, and renewal. If you haven't dedicated your life to Christ or if you feel a sense of distance from Him, now is the moment to make that leap of faith.

THE INVITATION TO SALVATION

The Bible tells us clearly how we can be saved and come into a relationship with God:

"If you declare with your mouth, 'Jesus is Lord,' and believe in your heart that God raised him from the dead, you will be saved. For it is with your heart that you believe and are justified, and it is with your mouth that you profess your faith and are saved." Romans 10:9-10

Salvation is not about what you've done or how good you've been. It's about what Jesus has already done for you. He died on the cross for your sins and rose again, defeating sin and death. All you have to do is accept this gift of grace.

A PRAYER OF SALVATION

If you're ready to give your life to Christ, you can pray this simple prayer from your heart:

Dear Jesus,

I know that I am a sinner and that I need Your forgiveness. I believe that You died for my sins and rose again so that I could have eternal life. Today, I choose to turn from my old ways and follow You. I declare that You are my Lord and Savior and invite You into my heart and life. Thank You for saving me and giving me a new purpose. Help me to live for You each day. In Your name, I pray. Amen.

If you prayed this prayer, know that all of heaven rejoiced over your decision! You are now a part of God's family, and your life has a new purpose and meaning.

NEXT STEPS IN YOUR FAITH JOURNEY

1. GET CONNECTED TO A CHURCH:
    - Find a local, Bible-believing church where you can grow your faith and build relationships with other believers.
2. START READING THE BIBLE:
    - Learn more about Jesus and His teachings by beginning with the Gospels (Matthew, Mark, Luke, and John).
3. PRAY REGULARLY:
    - Prayer is simply talking to God. Share your heart with Him daily and listen for His guidance.
4. SURROUND YOURSELF WITH ENCOURAGEMENT:
    - Seek mentors, friends, or small groups to support you in your walk with Christ.

WALKING IN YOUR P.U.R.P.O.S.E

As you rise to live out your purpose, remember the journey outlined in this book:

- **POSITION YOURSELF FOR GOD'S PLAN:** Align your life with His will and surrender your own.
- **UNDERSTAND YOUR IDENTITY IN CHRIST:** Know yourself and embrace your worth as God's child.
- **RECOGNIZE YOUR CALLING:** Discern the unique purpose God has given you.

- **PURSUE YOUR PURPOSE WITH PASSION:** Step forward with determination and enthusiasm.
- **OVERCOME OBSTACLES WITH FAITH:** Trust God to guide you through challenges.
- **STEP OUT IN BOLDNESS:** Take risks and move beyond your comfort zone for His glory.
- **EMBRACE YOUR ETERNAL IMPACT:** Live each day with the understanding that your life has significance beyond the here and now.

Each step brings you closer to the abundant life God has planned for you, a life of worth, purpose, and eternal impact.

A FINAL WORD OF ENCOURAGEMENT

As you close this book, let the words of Ephesians 3:20-21 be a banner over your life:

"Now to him who can do immeasurably more than all we ask or imagine, according to the power within us, to him be glory in the church and Christ Jesus throughout all generations, forever and ever! Amen."

God's power is at work within you, equipping you to fulfill your purpose and live a life that glorifies Him. Trust Him to do more than you could ever ask or imagine. Your worth is secure in Christ, and your impact will echo into eternity. It's time to rise, know your worth, and live boldly for His glory.

AFTERWORD

- Recap of the P.U.R.P.O.S.E. Framework
- Encouragement to Live with Worth
- A Prayer for Your Journey

Appendices

1. Reflection Questions for Personal Growth
2. Bible Verses for Daily Encouragement
3. Prayer Guide for Walking in Purpose

ACKNOWLEDGMENTS

Smith, J. (2025). Know Your Worth in Life: Unlocking Your Divine Purpose and Living with Spiritual Strength and Resilience. Day-N-Night Publishing, LLC.

Bible Verses Cited:

- Jeremiah 29:11
- Isaiah 55:8-9
- 1 Thessalonians 5:17
- Matthew 4:1-2
- Proverbs 27:17
- Psalm 46:10
- Romans 8:28
- 1 Peter 2:9
- 1 John 3:1
- Psalm 139:14
- 1 Corinthians 12:4-11
- 1 Corinthians 12:27
- Matthew 28:19-20
- Colossians 3:23
- Philippians 4:13
- James 1:2-4
- 2 Timothy 1:7
- Romans 5:3-5
- Proverbs 28:1
- Joshua 1:9
- Esther 4:16
- Acts 4:20

- Matthew 5:16
- Ephesians 3:20-21
- Romans 10:9-10

Additional Resources:

- Reflection Questions for Personal Growth
- Bible Verses for Daily Encouragement
- Prayer Guide for Walking in Purpose

www.ingramcontent.com/pod-product-compliance
Lightning Source LLC
Chambersburg PA
CBHW032100150426
43194CB00006B/596